Plants

Nicola Edwards

A&C Black · London

Some plants can be shaped into messages.

People have shaped these hedges to
spell out words from the Bible.

A gardener has planted these flowers to grow in the shape of a horse rider.

Gardeners have planted and shaped these hedges to make a maze. A maze is an outdoor puzzle. When you are in the middle of a maze it is difficult to see where you are going. Do you think you could find your way out of this maze?

Sometimes flowers can show that people are celebrating a special occasion.

The bridesmaids at this wedding are holding bouquets of flowers. The best man and the groom are wearing flowers called roses. Where else might you see flowers during a wedding?

Why do you think people give each other flowers on Valentine's Day?

These travellers are being presented with lotus blossoms to welcome them to their hotel.

People have given flowers to these ice-skaters to show that they have enjoyed the ice-dancing.

Plants are an important part of some religious festivals.

During the festival of Durga Puja, people who follow the Hindu religion hang strings of marigolds around a statue. The festival lasts for ten days. Each day people add another marigold to the string of flowers.

During this Jewish harvest festival, people build huts made of branches, twigs and leaves. This rabbi is leading the festival inside the hut, which is called a sukkah.

On Palm Sunday in this Christian church, the priest gives each person a cross made of palm leaves.

Plants can be used to remind us of something.

On Remembrance Sunday poppies remind us
of people who were killed in wartime.

The Canadian flag has
a maple leaf on it.
Can you see a maple
leaf in this photograph?
What does it tell you
about the airline?

What time of year do
these plants make you
think of?

Plants change with each season of the year. Look at the plants and trees in these pictures. Which season do you think each picture shows? Which is your favourite season?

Plants can sometimes give you clues about the part of the world that they come from.

Cacti grow in deserts where the weather is hot and dry. Plants lose water through their leaves. Cactus leaves have shrunk to spines to make it difficult for water to escape.

In this tropical rain forest the weather is hot and there is plenty of rain. The plants in the forest grow thick stems and huge leaves.

Plants can show when people have not been looking after them.

Plants need light and water in order to grow and be healthy. Which of these plants has been kept in a dark cupboard without being watered?
How can you tell?

The trees in this photograph
have been harmed by acid rain.

These trees are growing by the
side of a busy road. The children
are wiping the leaves of the trees
with damp cotton wool. The fumes
from car exhausts have made the
leaves dirty.

Plants can give messages to insects.

Insects help to spread pollen
from one flower to another.
Pollen is needed to make
seeds which will grow
into new plants.

Flowers can attract
insects to them . . .

. . . by giving out
a strong smell . . .

. . . and by the colour of their petals.

The shape of this foxglove's petals and the pattern of spots on them guide bees to the pollen in the centre of the flower.

17

People use messages to sell plants.

The signs on this market stall show people how much each type of flower costs.

These children are visiting a florist's shop.
A florist is someone who sells flowers.
The children are choosing a bunch of flowers to send to their granny for her birthday.

Can you see any messages that tell you about flowers in this picture?

This person is buying plants
at a garden centre.

The label on each plant can show you:

the place where it was bought

the name of the plant

how to look after it

how much it costs

BLOOMS
Garden
Centre

Flaming Katy
(Kalenchoe)
Place on a sunny
window-sill.
Water compost
and wait until
compost is dry
before watering
again.

£2.50

The instructions on this packet of seeds tell you how to grow some cress plants.

CRESS

Growing instructions
1. Put some compost into a pot.
2. Sprinkle some cress seeds on top.
3. Cover them with a thin layer of compost.
4. Put the pot on a window sill where it will have plenty of light.
5. Water it regularly to keep the soil damp.

After a few days the seeds begin to sprout!

Have you ever tried to grow a plant?

Index

For parents and teachers

The aim of the *Messages* series is to help build confidence in children who are just beginning to read, by encouraging them to make meaning from the different kinds of signs and symbols which surround them in their everyday lives. Here are some suggestions for follow-up activities which extend the ideas introduced in the book.

Pages 2/3 The children could make their own floral message, such as a greeting, which they could plan by sticking scrunched-up tissue paper on to card. They could use bulbs or plants to create a message in the school garden, or they could sprinkle cress seeds on to a tray of damp cotton wool to create an indoor message. You could arrange a visit to a local maze and, back at school, draw up a design for a maze using ideas suggested by the children.

Pages 4/5 Children could talk about occasions when they have worn, carried or given flowers, for instance, at a wedding or on Mothering Sunday. They could make a birthday or Valentine's Day card with a bouquet of paper flowers on the front.

Pages 6/7 Flowers and plants form an important part of many religious festivals. The Hindu festival of Durga Puja is also known as Navaratri, or nine nights, during which the different manifestations of the goddess Devi are worshipped. An oil lamp is kept burning in every Hindu household for the duration of the festival. A string of marigolds is hung around the lamp and a fresh flower is added to the string on each day of the festival. The Jewish festival of Sukkot is also known as the

Feast of the Tabernacles. The festival commemorates the Israelites' 40-year journey through the wilderness and the temporary dwellings they erected along the way. Several of the plants which feature in the festival have a symbolic significance, including the etrog (citrus) and the lulav (palm branch). Palm crosses given to Christian worshippers on Palm Sunday commemorate Christ's entry into Jerusalem riding on a donkey, when his path was strewn with palm leaves. Find out about the significance of plants in other religious festivals.

Pages 8/9 Collect some plants or pictures of plants and ask the children what each plant makes them think of (for example, a time of year, a place they visited on holiday). You could talk about the wider significance of each plant (they might be historical or national symbols, or used as company logos).

Pages 10/11 Look at the ways in which poets and artists have responded to the seasons. The children could make their own pictures with paint, paper, fabric and dried leaves and flowers to show what each season means to them. They might show how the natural world changes colour or how the weather affects the type of clothes they wear. A pile of books can be used to make a simple flower press – lay the plant or flower between sheets of absorbent paper, which should be replaced every couple of days.

Pages 12/13 Collect some plants or pictures of plants to show how different species have adapted to extreme conditions. You could talk about plants which provide us with food and other products, such as paper and medicines, and where in the world these are grown.

Pages 14/15 Talk to the children about other ways in which plants can show that they've been neglected – for example, by losing their leaves or shrivelling up. You could set up a series of simple experiments to show the children how a plant will respond to poor conditions such as insufficient light or water.

Pages 16/17 You could talk about how some plants such as thistles or stinging nettles use their appearance to deter animals which may otherwise try to eat them. Many poisonous plants look completely harmless – you could work out a code of safe practice with the children to be used when looking at wild flowers and plants.

Pages 18/19 Set up a market stall or florist's shop in the classroom using flowers which the children have made themselves out of card and paper. They could write price labels for each type of flower and design posters to encourage people to buy a bouquet. There are opportunities for role-play activities.

Pages 20/21 Take the children on a walk around the school grounds or a local park; you could talk about the shape and colour of the different flowers and plants as well as the effects of seasonal change. Perhaps you could arrange for a gardener to talk about planting and maintaining the flowers. Take photographs to record how the greenery changes during the year.

Pages 22/23 The children could grow plants from seed in empty yoghurt pots or plastic tumblers, perhaps using seeds and compost donated by parents. They could keep a daily record of any changes they observe.